FROM ORDINARY TO ENTREPRENEUR

Your Billion-dollar idea into action

Amit Kumar Jha

From Ordinary to Entrepreneur Copyright © 2018 by Amit Kumar Jha. All Rights Reserved.

All rights reserved. No part of this book may be reproduced in any form or by any electronic or mechanical means including information storage and retrieval systems, without permission in writing from the author. The only exception is by a reviewer, who may quote short excerpts in a review.

Cover designed by Amit Kumar Jha

This book has been written with an intention to help the youth in flourishing their goals as an entrepreneur. The book also provides all necessary information that one may need.

Feel free to write us at talk@amitKumarJha.com

Amit Kumar Jha
Visit my website at www.Amitkumarjha.com

Dedicated to:
My Parents who stood by me when the world was against

*One thing that you can always be guaranteed is that,
If you go for a Start-Up you will never see the failure.
Either you succeed or you learn what to do next and succeed.*

ABOUT THE AUTHOR

Amit Kumar Jha is an Indian Entrepreneur, blogger, Writer, motivational speaker, trainer, programmer and web developer. He was born on 10th October 1986 and has started coding since his sixth standard. Amit Kumar Jha is also the founder of WEBNext Labs and iPehchan. He has also received Governor's Medal for his Adventurous activities and received a large number of rewards throughout his career.

Amit Kumar Jha believes in the fact that no other thing can prevent a person from being a great entrepreneur or a programmer if you have the desire to be one. He also conducts training and seminars to help people become an entrepreneur. At his school, he creates awesome programmers out of people who claim to not have seen computer before.

https://www.amitkumarjha.com

CONTENTS

About the Author 5
Introduction 8
    who is an Entrepreneur? 9
    Are you an Entrepreneur Material? 11
    What do you need to be an Entrepreneur? 12
Life of an Entrepreneur 15
    Support from Family and Friends 16
    Response from the Society 18
    Bank's attitude towards Entrepreneurs 18
    Importance of Failure 19
    Entrepreneur's attitude towards failure 20
    The right moment for success 22
Being an Entrepreneur 24
    General traits 24
    Important habits to adopt as an Entrepreneur 28
Stages of Successful Business 34
    Milestone 1: Start your business. 35
    Milestone 2: Moment of No-return 35
    Milestone 3: Prototype to Product 36
    Milestone 4: Transformation from Innovators to Businessmen 37
    Some advice to remember 38
What drives an Entrepreneur 41
    Passion 41
    Motivation 42
Internet – a power tool for entrepreneurs 44
    The WEB Entrepreneurs 45

- Internet for expansion 45
- Internet for Marketing 46
- Internet for communication 47
- Internet for knowledge 48

Be with the right people 49

- People who motivate 50
- People with experience 51
- People with knowledge 51
- People who can join 52

Business Entities & Associated Laws 54

- Types of Business EntiTies 55
- Regulatory requirements and statutory bodies involved in starting a business 59

Protecting Your Business 62

- Intellectual Property 63
- Why protect the Brand name and logo? 64
- How to protect your intellectual property? 66

The Billion Dollar Idea 68

Conclusion 71

INTRODUCTION

Understanding Entrepreneurship

Today everyone wishes to live the lifestyle of a successful entrepreneur but people often tend to overlook the fact that they need to be an Entrepreneur in order to live such a life. This book guides you on how to start the life of an entrepreneur, develop the essential habits and finally be the one you always wish to be. Yes, this is your time when you get started with the billion-dollar idea and live the life, you always wished to live. You may be from an ordinary family and may have been living simply till now, but living an ordinary life is not your destiny. We all get a chance to create our own destiny and it's just about implementing the right idea in a right way with the resources that are available to you. You may also find situations when you feel that you are out of resources to execute your plans and this is the book that will make you ready enough to face all the challenges that may come in your way. But before that let's learn a little about how is it being an Entrepreneur.

WHO IS AN ENTREPRENEUR?

This is the most common question in today's world and it always brings out different answers and explanations when asked to different people. All the answers are almost same but answered in a different way. We would, however, summarize a general definition that will explain the true meaning of an entrepreneur. An Entrepreneur is someone who identifies a problem in the current world, finds a scalable solution to the problem, and does everything to implement it, no matter how. Entrepreneurs have the vision to change the way we see the world today, but not only he has this dream but he also chases his dream till he finally gets it done. It's about people who are ready to risk everything that they have to achieve their one goal that has the potential to change the life of many. The life of an entrepreneur is much more different than compared to an ordinary person. It has a lot of moments where one has to undergo long sleepless nights, frustration, rejections and all such things but the final payback is highly rewarding and is much more beautiful than what one can imagine.

There is a famous saying about entrepreneurs. It reads like

"Entrepreneurship is about living a few years of your life which no one would so that you can live the rest of your life which no one could."

In the initial stage of every entrepreneurial journey, there will be situations when no one is ready to believe and everyone is ready to reject the entrepreneur. However, it is the most important characteristics of an entrepreneur is that rejection only makes them, even more, stronger and experienced. The best part of being an entrepreneur is that there is no failure in the life of a true Entrepreneur. Let me explain you with a very exciting example. Suppose you go to buy a property, say an apartment. You invest your time, effort and money and finally, you buy the apartment. But what if the property is not what you were looking for. You don't buy it. right! But at the same time, you also don't need to stop your search. You keep on searching till you get the right thing. Similarly, an entrepreneur keeps up and takes every possible measure to achieve his goal. Either they succeed or they gain experience and keep trying until they become successful.

There is also a very common practice that sees now a day. Every person who is not a professional or an employed person tries to call himself an entrepreneur. Buying such a habit is not recommended as that is not what one wants as an entrepreneur. Entrepreneurs get real satisfaction by the success they achieve and not by what they call themselves.

It's not enough to be a star with the potential to be a superstar. Underestimating self-potential is the first node of an endless chain of mistakes.

ARE YOU AN ENTREPRENEUR MATERIAL?

This is a doubt that may stop the very potential person from reaching the goal. Never cultivate such a feeling inside you as that's in no way less than the rust. Yes, you may or may not be a born entrepreneur. You may not even come from a business family and it may even be that you have zero experience of what business is about but they all seem worthless when you identify your real passion and the desire to live the life of an entrepreneur. That one fire in you can burn all the negatives and barriers and make your free. Every person who is motivated and a self-starter is a potential entrepreneur material. You can push and drive a car, bus, a cart but you cannot push and drive a train, a rocket, a jet or a Ship. Similarly, employees can be pushed to do something but Entrepreneurs need to be self-motivated. They just need to have that flame in them. Yes, the right tool, training, and guidance is something that is required for a better success.

Now! I can guarantee that you are a solid entrepreneur material and you are meant to succeed in life or else you would not have been reading till here. You have a desire to be the next great one and here are the practices, the ways and the guidance that will make you super successful.

Let's start step by step on how you can train the Entrepreneur in you for excellence and live the life you always wanted to. Some get it in a tough way and some go through the toughest. It's the situation when the common people quit and entrepreneurs make the difference. Life of an entrepreneur is never as easy as it looks like, no matter how lucky you are. Entrepreneurship is not about one-time luck, but it's about persistence. We will also discuss the billion-dollar idea that you can implement in starting your own start-up where success in guaranteed and rewards are high.

If you don't do what you love, You have no right to say what you love to do.

WHAT DO YOU NEED TO BE AN ENTREPRENEUR?

Now, here we have a very good news that you already have everything that you need to be an entrepreneur. Some of them are known to you and some are unknown, but the fact cannot be denied that you have everything you need to be an entrepreneur. You also have a lot of ideas that can be utilized to build a successful company. It's just that you need to be made aware of your powers and specialties.

Now before we proceed further, let's just make a quick assessment and find out if there is the seed of entrepreneurism in you. Ask yourself the following questions.

- Do you feel that there are things missing in this world and this world can be made even better by making necessary changes or inventions?
- Would you love to go ahead and solve a problem in the lives of people instead of sitting back and complaining about everything?
- Do you wish to be your own boss and at the same time wish to provide employment to others?
- Do you wish to be remembered even after many years from now?
- Do you think that you can fight for your passion beyond any limit and make things work no matter what the situation is?
- Do you ask yourself about what extraordinary you can achieve and get bored with a regular lifestyle?

If you feel that you are answering in yes to more than one questions above, then you are already an entrepreneur. However, Not all entrepreneurs reach the success point. Some keep trying and learning throughout their life and that's not because they do have the right passion and mindset, but they miss out the right practices and guidance. It is said:

Small steps in right direction can help you reach your goal but steps in the wrong direction can take you miles away from your goal

Thus, you need to know the direction while taking every step.

Entrepreneurial life is tough and risky and probably we can add all such words to this sentence, but if you meet an entrepreneur and ask them about how they feel about these, they would just say that they love it. The risk in life is like salt in food. If you don't add it, you eat tastelessly. The life of an entrepreneur is also very exciting if seen through the eyes of an entrepreneur. We have been discussing a lot about what the life of an entrepreneur is like but, all you need to know that this topic is like an ocean. People see from the shore or from the ship. And entrepreneurs are like divers in the sea. As it's only the divers who take the risk to jump in and finally explore the beauty of the ocean entrepreneurs take the risk and enjoy the real moments of life.

Age, gender, locality, certification and nothing else matters when it comes to building a successful company. All you need is the fire within and the passion to do something that others can only imagine of.

This life is full of risk but it's always worth taking the risk. In the following chapters, we will talk about what you should practice, what to avoid, some technical training, and the guidance to be successful. Finally, we will get into the discussion about the million-dollar idea and the way to build your successful company.

LIFE OF AN ENTREPRENEUR

Time to get prepared

Entrepreneurs do have a specific lifestyle and it is so different from common people that it often makes common people confused. The only problem with the lifestyle is that it's highly diversified and is tough for others to understand and relate. Some entrepreneurs go to sleep at around 5 am in the morning while some wake up at 5 am. Some sleep at night and some sleep during the day. There are few who go to sleep after a few days. So, if you see properly, the feature is that their lifestyle is not centered around the daily tasks like sleeping, eating, and such things. The lifestyle is centered around the task that they are doing.

Creating a startup is different from doing a job and is always an awesome experience. The startup can always be compared to your baby and you are the one to decide everything and Not anybody else. You have to take care of it like your baby and in the long term it will pay you back and fulfill your dreams. It will also take care of you when you get old. Now imagine the situation of a person, who has a new-born baby. The baby may demand the parent's attention at any time and for any amount of time and there is no timetable in the world that can explain when a baby will start crying. So is the case with a start-up. You need to take care of it and you can never be sure about how many hours a day you need to dedicate to it. With a startup, you start living life of a new-born baby's parent who spends sleepless nights and is still ready for the next day.

SUPPORT FROM FAMILY AND FRIENDS

Yes! Entrepreneurs are human beings too and like anybody else, they too have a family and friends of their own. But the most painful part is that the story is not the same. Let me explain this in a little more detail.

As an entrepreneur, you will find a family that can easily be divided into two segments. The supportive ones and the ones standing against you. Usually, your mom will be the only one who will be on your side. Your spouse may or may not be on this team. All the other members will be standing against you. Every member shall have a different advice for you about how you should listen to them, stop spoiling your life, and make your life better by getting into a regular job. There will also be people who will be ready to predict how you will be unsuccessful in your future and will also demonstrate, how Mr. x and Mr. y had failed. However, the scenario is not always the same. When the father is the leader of the opponent team in most of the cases, it has also been seen that father proves to be the most supportive person in the family.

There is another problem that you may face in your family. Suppose you are about to do some work for which demands you to stay awake and work hard for say something around 50 hours. And during this, all you can do is the basic important stuff like going to the washroom. Apart from that, there is no time for bathing, changing clothes and so you avoid it. Since the time is less, you may even eat something fast instead of regular meals. Here as an entrepreneur, you have a perfect plan and you know that the task is more important than anything and you need to do it first. But you will find your family members trying to stop you and forcing you to sleep or do regular tasks. This is also the reasons why most of the entrepreneurs are found staying away from their family.

Talking about friends, Entrepreneurs find it tough time finding the right fit friends. You will have some friends who think that they are not yet successful and so they will keep themselves away from you while there will be friends who are working in some branded MNC and they think that you and your startup is too irrelevant to them and so they too keep away from you. Very few will be there who will love your company and support you, whereas there will be a lot who will enjoy giving you examples and suggestions and mostly demotivating tips.

As an entrepreneur, it is your duty to choose the right company and groups to be with so that you don't get lost in your journey. We will discuss in details about selecting the right people to be within the upcoming chapters.

RESPONSE FROM THE SOCIETY

The society shall always be ready to criticize you in every possible way. There will be a time when the society will consider you as a failure and will declare that you are the most miserable person, and will also explain to you that ordinary people are not meant to be at that level of success. Similarly, when you struggle and become successful, then the same bunch of people will say that you were born to be so and in fact, they will also claim that you were successful since your birth and you never had a hard time.

BANK'S ATTITUDE TOWARDS ENTREPRENEURS

This is the most heart-breaking statement but it's a fact that Banks hate entrepreneurs and their startup. Someone has perfectly said that bank is an organization that lends you money when you need it the least. As an entrepreneur, you will surely come to a situation where you will need some sort of investment. Now the first place that comes to mind, while thinking about a loan is the bank. However, unlike the Angel Investors, banks are not interested in any kind of risk and so they will behave as if you don't exist in this world. We will talk about the Angel Investors soon in the upcoming chapters.

IMPORTANCE OF FAILURE

This is something that plays the most import role on the part of an entrepreneurial journey. Now one would think about how can failure be an important part of one's life? In fact, you may also wonder what if someone finds success at the very first attempt? And is it compulsory to fail to be an entrepreneur? There are a lot of questions that may come to your mind when I say that failure is important.

Let me give you an example. Suppose you are cooking a delicious recipe. It may be that the food is perfectly cooked when you check it for the first time. But there can be a situation when you check and you find that you need to cook more. What do you do? You keep cooking till it's complete. Now, will you call the events of checking as a failure? Absolutely not. Similarly, when you are doing something, you may need to take multiple attempts before the task is completed.

In many countries, there is a concept called failure where if you are unable to complete a task on the first attempt, you are stamped as a failure. This tag of failure may start demotivating you and will reduce your performance. In the entrepreneurial culture, there is no such term as a failure. We call them experience. It's only the experienced people who have seen the other side and knows how to react when the adverse situation comes. If you visit the Silicon Valley, you will find that failures who did not give-up are given more importance than the people who just achieved success at the very first attempt.

ENTREPRENEUR'S ATTITUDE TOWARDS FAILURE

Entrepreneurs are getting stronger and stronger every time failure touches them. They never stop or give up if failure comes to them. Instead, they get back up once again and keeps getting back up till the success is achieved. Every time a plan seems like not working, an entrepreneur modifies the plan and strikes back again.

> *You may Forget your failures, but don't forget the lesson it gave you.*

Now you may not fall down after a failure and nor you should quit in adverse situations. But you should always fear the failure. It's your fear of failure that keeps you with the success. So, what we finally summaries that we should not panic if the failure comes, but we should always take sufficient steps so that failure never comes.

If you don't fear the failure, then probably success is not important for you

---

It's the reaction to failure that makes an entrepreneur different from others. But remember one important thing. Fear of Failure should not stop you from taking the risk but should stop you from stopping. You should have the fear of the consequences of failure so that you never even dream to fail. success comes only to those who sacrifice their comfort zone and take the extra risk. Remember! the only difference between winners and losers is that one extra step. It's the moment when other feel like quitting after too many attempts but successful entrepreneurs keep taking one more and another more step to success is achieved. You may never know how close you are to your success

More importantly, Failure is a kind of vaccination. It may give you a temporary trouble, but in the long term, it teaches you about how to stay strong and fight the situation. Experts say that, before being super successful, you must have failed one or more company, but if you haven't any then this is the company that you are going to fail. Now, this should not instigate you to go ahead and ruin your current startup, but it just means that every time a difficult situation comes to you, you get more and more stronger and experienced.

THE RIGHT MOMENT FOR SUCCESS.

I have seen many people who wait for the right moment to come and I have also seen people who claim that someone became successful when he stroked at the very right moment. Never buy such an idea.

What gives success to an entrepreneur is few months or even years of hard work, lots of sacrifice, sleepless nights, cashless wallets, bitter advice from people, lots of study, too many attempts and that one final attempt which starts a new segment of their life from when he or she starts glittering and becomes everyone's dreams idol. People see the moment when an entrepreneur gets his success but fails to see the background tasks and home works done to achieve the success. Is harvesting the crop the only step for farming? Is showing, plowing the land, protecting against cattle and watering all just show off? All steps may not bring a visible output, but every step counts when it's about success.

Entrepreneurship is like jumping off a very high cliff and the building your own plane or parachute, whatever you wish, on your way down and mostly without any instruction. All you need to know is that you have to do it no matter how. Every moment is the very right moment to start your startup as you can never be sure of whether someone else will invent the same thing before you. The only thing that matters is who does it first. So, waiting for a right moment to start can prove fatal so it is always the best idea to start first. We will also learn about how to protect your ideas from being stolen in the upcoming chapters.

There may be situations when it would feel like there's no scope for what you have planned. Never give up as an entrepreneur, it is you who has to find out how to do the impossible as that is what you can do and others can't. Ronaldo and Messi are famous players but are they what they are just because they score goals? No. They are what they are because they score a goal even when the situation is impossible. That's how an entrepreneur solves a problem with his ideas.

Remember!
The easier things you choose to do in life, the less happy and satisfied you become on its completion.

BEING AN ENTREPRENEUR

The characteristics that you need to grow in yourself

There are a bunch of characteristics seen in entrepreneurs that make them different from others and it's not compulsory that all of them must be present in you but you must try to have most of them so that you make the most. There also exist some more qualities which have not been covered. Reason being that entrepreneurs have a very flexible schedule and they are highly unpredictable. Thus, any set of characteristics can never fit them all.

GENERAL TRAITS

They are self-starter
Entrepreneurs are self-starters and self-motivators. You cannot motivate a person to be an entrepreneur unless the feeling

comes to him from inside. But once the feeling comes in, that person cannot be stopped at any cost. Yes, a proper guidance may prove beneficial and might bring success faster.

They take action
Entrepreneurs just need a concept in mind to get started. They don't need a detailed strategy to start their plan. Instead of planning they invent as they proceed further on their journey.

They feel insecure about success
Entrepreneurs always have a feeling of insecurity when it comes about their success. This feeling makes them hyper-focused on what they do. This feeling makes success more guaranteed.

They are Crafty
You may not have all the resources that you need to set up your business and keep the things going. Now, this should not be able to stop you from proceeding. You need to figure out things. It's not about having a lot of resources but it's about being resourceful with all what you have.

They are obsessed about cash flow
Entrepreneurs are highly obsessed while spending their cash. They know that however big or small a company is; cash is

required to run the company for one more day. This is the thing to worry about.

They get into hot water
Whatever be the scenario, Entrepreneurs are never happy with it. Moreover, entrepreneurs are more likely to ask for forgiveness than permission. They cannot wait for a long time to get the permission to do something. Instead, they begin and if required they may apologize later for not taking permission.

They are fearless
When common people avoid the risk, entrepreneurs seek potential. In some ways, entrepreneurs are ultimate optimists as they believe that their time and investment will eventually pay off.

They can't sit still
Finding an entrepreneur sitting idle and doing nothing is a tough thing. They are highly energized and always eager to do some work. You will find entrepreneurs busy working in the office when their employees have left long back.

They are malleable
As an entrepreneur, do not be open to only one acceptable outcome from what you are doing. Smart entrepreneurs

consistently evolve tweaking their business concepts in response to market feedback.

They are naval gazing
As an entrepreneur, you also need to be comfortable with the process of evaluating and modifying your own performance. Always take feedback from your clients and customers.

They are motivated by challenges
When confronted by problems, entrepreneurs rise to the occasion. It is the challenges that motivate entrepreneurs and make them work harder.

They consider themselves an outsider
Where ever they go, entrepreneurs are not always accepted. They are often rejected for being different from the majority in some or the other way. This makes them work harder.

They recover quickly
Just because successful entrepreneurs have more energy and they proceed faster, they fail a lot and very often. But the best part is that they don't sit back or cry. They immediately get up and start with the next big thing.

They fulfill needs

People recognize marketplace holes but the true entrepreneurs take them from the cocktail napkin to reality. Entrepreneurs think of a way to fix it and takes steps to fix it. In fact, they are innovators who live to change the world for the better.

They work and play hard

They do fall down but they immediately pick themselves up until they get it right. Some people in the history tried 10 times, some tried a hundred times to get success. A true entrepreneur will keep trying no matter how many time till they get success.

They have the ability to take action, even after uncertainty.

Entrepreneurs do have the guts to take a decision and plan the next move when the common people stop. They are believed to work and take an important decision even under maximum stress.

IMPORTANT HABITS TO ADOPT AS AN ENTREPRENEUR.

There are some habits which if made a part of your life, will lead to more success as an entrepreneur. You may not adopt all of them but any amount that you can be highly helpful. Entrepreneurs do need to have what makes them ready for an entrepreneurial journey.

Surround yourself with advisors.
Get surrounded by smarter people and listen to ideas that aren't yours. True entrepreneurs don't hire yes men. Instead, they talk to those with experience and conduct thorough research gathering much information as they can on the subject to make an informed decision.

Make partnership with big brands.
When you set up your startup, it's not possible to be a multi-billion-dollar business in the first few days. But attempts can be made to look like one. Try to make partner with big brands. This partnership can be of any form. Use their logos with your logo which will make your logo too look like a big brand. You can also explain, that your company is small and growing, but you do deal with large corporations.

Improve your speed of implementation.
Live your life like as if there is no tomorrow. What has to be done, must be done today. Always be in a hurry. You never know what might happen tomorrow. The new law may be enforced, people may change, a different solution may come in

the market, or maybe your competitors will start something that you wanted to.

Realize the importance of time.
You will never find entrepreneurs wasting time. Yes, entrepreneurs are mostly flexible about time and their timings to do things is never fixed, but whatever they do, they can never be found wasting time. Try to utilize time as much as you can for productive purposes.

Take care of your health.
This may seem like out of the context but this is equally important. Since you are going to be the key person of your company, you need to keep your body and mind healthy. Yes, you may find entrepreneurs eating junk, not sleeping and doing such stuff. But whatever you do, avoid getting ill as that will slow you down. Understand how much your body can take and strain accordingly. If required train your body to work more.

Read as much as you can.
Here we are not talking about some academic education, nor some novel or a comic book. There is a popular saying, if you want to lead, you need to read. Read anything that you find interesting regarding your work and passion. You are not expected to each and everything about all the departments of your work, but you must know at least the basics about everything that is related I anyway to your work.

Stay away from the negatives.
You will find some negative people during your career, whose primary mission in life is to blame people, society, government, nature, country, in fact, everything. They never take any kind of risk. They just like to sing the song about how many times they failed and how they tried. They have no interest in their success. They even stop others from taking any sort of risk. If they find something good happening, they have a problem in that too. Such people can never help you grow. They can only lower your motivation and there should be no place for such people in the life of an entrepreneur.

Look big unless you are really big.
If you try to keep yourself to the ground level from the beginning and plan to grow as your business grows, probable, that will not be a very wise idea. You will find people not paying attention to you. All you need to do is present yourself as something very big, someone very successful and beyond their reach. This will create a great boost. Now your fake showoff will soon turn into reality and you will not need a fake makeover anymore.

Look big unless you really grow big, once you are big, you will automatically look big.

Just remember! You need to look like big. Don't look big and forget your motive or cheat people or do such crazy stuff. Also, try to look big, but don't create an extra fake impression like the MLM leaders. People can understand.

Learn from other's mistakes.

Remember! We don't have enough time to do all the mistakes by ourselves and learn from them. So, it is always a better option to learn from the mistakes of others. But most important, understand why it became a mistake and also find out about what could have been done to avoid and recover the mistake.

Keep out of Comfort Zone

Remember! If you are sable, then it doesn't only mean that you are not falling, but it also means that you are not rising. Entrepreneurs know that being stagnant takes you nowhere. Thus, Entrepreneurs keep themselves away from the comfort zone and love to be in the risk zone where you hold a good chance of falling but the chances of rising very high are equal, or sometimes even better.

Never gamble for success

I will always keep telling you that you should not let any chance go and should keep doing anything that you can without giving up. Now, this statement will be a little different. You should take the risk only if you are prepared to take it. If you are not ready, you should wait and prepare instead of showing extra confidence. Never Gamble for success.

Learn and implement leadership skills.

An entrepreneur always needs to play as a leader. They need to start the thing, build their team and manage the team in every rise and fall and be an example for the team. Some people are born with leadership skills however that skill needs to be polished. Now if you are kind of a person, who is born without leadership skills there are chances that you can develop those skills in you.

STAGES OF SUCCESSFUL BUSINESS

Make Sure your business reaches these steps

Every business needs to follow some specific strategies in order to reach the success. Mind that success is not a destination, but a journey. Maintaining the success achieved is equally important as reaching the success level. Your business may have a plan or you may keep building your plan as you proceed, but these are the important milestones that you need to achieve in order to keep your business up and running. Too many startups are born every day while only a few manage to survive in the long run. Reason being, the ones who go out of existence are the ones who missed to pass the below four major milestones.

MILESTONE 1: START YOUR BUSINESS.

All of us are very good at dreaming a great business, it's plan, products, and the success. We also often dream up to its return, uniqueness and its scope in the market. However, we all somehow miss the only very important thing that matters and that is to start the business. Remember, the only thing that goes down the history is that you started your business and if you don't start, everything is wasted.

MILESTONE 2: MOMENT OF NO-RETURN

Most of the times it is seen that entrepreneurs often tend to get attracted to something else or get distracted by something else and forget their main motive that they had started with. So, after you have played around a while with your idea or product, try to reach a point of no return. Be it your family, friends, society, rival, government, loan or anything else, but that should prevent you from giving up. Reach the point in business, where you have no option to give or quit. The only option that should remain with you should be to proceed with your business and be successful.

Mostly what we see is that entrepreneurs often get frustrated with the task they initially started. It is also seen that friend and family demotivate by explaining the circumstances that may occur in the journey. Finally, the entrepreneur to starts believing that the decision they took was somehow wrong. Now I would say that if this was wrong, the decision would not have been taken. It's the entrepreneurs, who have the ability to see the real opportunity. Entrepreneurs make a difference and are able to change the world just because, they find an opportunity where others find risk and impossibility. Thus, entrepreneurs need to pass this point so that nothing would be able to stop them from executing what they planned.

MILESTONE 3: PROTOTYPE TO PRODUCT

With a startup in mind, every one of us first tends to build a rapid prototype in order to make their vision clear in front of them, among their partners, to the world as well as to the investors. What happens, is we concentrate on the problem-solving part and forget about the rest. Now with the number of resources available in the market, building a prototype is very easy. However, prototypes are not reliable in the long run and at the same time not scalable.

Thus, if you try to enter the market with a prototype, you will soon burn your own bridges and destroy all your future scope in the market by your own hands. Thus, you are required to get to the product that can both be scalable and reliable. Yes, it may be the scenario where you have the idea that you are working on but the technical or business part is limited. In that case, you can hire an employee or better than that take a co-founder who completes you, finds interest in your business and comes into an agreement with you. Yes, you can always take steps and precaution so that the idea is not stolen.

MILESTONE 4: TRANSFORMATION FROM INNOVATORS TO BUSINESSMEN

We all love to create things and we fall in love with what we create. This is completely normal, but what is not normal is the moment when we expect our users to love our product the same way. We cannot ask our users to love what we make, but we can surely make what people love to have. We also need to understand the market, our customers, their requirements, their urgency, the market valuation and a lot of statistics on how our movement should be. Instead of technology-driven, we need to market-driven, thus this is the right time when you replace your tech CEO by a business-minded CEO. This does not mean that you need to leave your seat and offer it to someone else. It just means that you need to change your mindset from that of an innovator to that of a real businessman. In case you don't have the ability or understanding of the market, you can always hire a CEO who can report you the details. What matters at the day's end is your business needs to generate revenue from the market to survive in the long run.

Once you find your product sufficient to be delivered in the market, you need to start understanding the situations and modify your next business moves accordingly. As a founder, you must read and gather more information about your industry, the latest trends and most importantly, your competitors, unless you are far ahead of everyone else. By this, I am not advising you to copy your competitors or learn from them. I am also not asking you to compare yourself or do what they do. It is just to see that your company do not lag behind the others.

SOME ADVICE TO REMEMBER

If you have reached the above four milestones and you actively keep reviewing your business, then it's sure that your company will make a good name in the long run and survive for a very long time. I thought you may like some advice, so here are some advice that might help you in the long run.

You and your company may be interesting, but however interesting you are, you need to pinpoint to your specific customer. You cannot go in general waiting for your sale. Know the first name and the last name of the person who is going to write you a cheque, just because, he/she really needs your product. This is what I always find missing. While your product may be open to many, or sometimes all, you need to know the major group who are your active customers.

Second most important thing is that people wait for their product to be perfect before taking them into the market, which in fact never happens. Don't wait for the time to make your product perfect as that is a very dangerous trap. Go to the market with a minimum viable product and get the feel. Se the market's reaction to your product and then evolve accordingly. It may be that by the time you make your product perfect, the trends change or it may even be that what you think to be perfect maybe not then. Scoring a goal in the empty field or normal market condition does not make you a champion, game-changing champions score out of impossible situations. So, learn to score from imperfect market conditions as the perfect market may not be found ever.

Last but not the least, we do find companies falling in love with their tech or product which may stand problematic. Sometimes a better product becomes available in the market and you miss to find it. Your mission should be to be market driven and retain your customers. In such a scenario, it will be a very wise idea to borrow someone else's product to satisfy your customers while you can work a little extra to make your own product. After all what you are after is the market and not the medal of having used your product or technology. Just don't get too emotional about your technology.

Entrepreneurship involves a lot of hard work where you need to be careful on a lot of things and often get involved into multitasking but that's worth a shot. After all, when you start a company you bring about a lot of changes in the world, but the best part is that you give employment to people, and help them earn and keep their family alive. This is a great experience and the satisfaction that it brings is above everything.

If you jump up to reach the stars, you may not catch one
But be sure, you will never end up with a hand full of mud.

---

* * *

WHAT DRIVES AN ENTREPRENEUR

The fuel that drives an Entrepreneur

There are a few things that drive an entrepreneur in the long run out of which passion plays a very important role. Lack of passion can prove fatal during this journey and sometimes may be the reason for drastic failure. However, motivation is also required and that has to be from the within. There has to certain fuel to drive the vehicle of entrepreneurship and more the fuel, more are the chances of success. Here are some of them that make the difference.

PASSION

passion is something that has to be present while you are founding a company. If you ever try to get into a business that has no relation to you personally, then there is a maximum chance that you may give up doing that business and hop to something else. The initial journey of entrepreneurship is very tough and the toughness may go beyond anyone's imagination.

The toughness may vary from sleepless nights to restless days. There can be long unpaid working hours and without any money in the wallet. You may have to undergo a lot of hardship and in the meantime, there will be a lot of people trying to demotivate you. Rejections and failures would be your shadow and life would seem like lost. Under such a situation, if you don't have passion, you are likely to give up in the long run.

Passion also plays a very important role because, in the entrepreneurial journey, you need to do things that might pay you after a very long time or even it may be that, that particular thing may never pay. For example, we work in the office, that pays but we wear neat and clean clothes, that does not pay but that has to be done. Similarly, in every startup, we need to perform some additional tasks that have to be performed but will not pay off directly. Also, we need to learn a lot and be persistent at what we do and that is not possible without passion.

MOTIVATION

The ultimate goal for any business is to make a monetary profit as that is the only thing that can keep the business up and running, but what motivates an entrepreneur is rarely money. This is a very strange statement but stands to be the greatest truth. Entrepreneurs do what they do just because they enjoy doing so. The greatest motivation is that they enjoy the lifestyle of an entrepreneur. They love to create things and solving a real-life problem brings them the maximum satisfaction. If you take a closer look at the life of entrepreneurs, you will be amazed to see that most of them invented what they did just to solve their personal problem. They found a problem in the world, found a solution and started using it. Then they realized that even the world can use it and this and they do it as it just makes them extra happy to find that the world enjoys their creation. Yes, they do make money but satisfaction is what comes first. They want to be their own boss and bring about a change in the system for its betterment. Entrepreneurs are also seen to be fascinated by name and fame. Some might be after building their lost reputation while others might be after creating their reputation. Some even just love to make their living in a way where they can serve others and their passion at the same time.

Entrepreneurial life is something that's very un-predicted and different from others and in such a scenario, where there is no guidance, more struggle and unknown tomorrow, it is tough to survive without a motivation. Money is not just enough to keep them intact with what they do. If Money would have been then they would have been doing a nine to five regular job making money. Instead, they choose to work days and night coz that's for something which is above the value of money.

* * *

INTERNET – A POWER TOOL FOR ENTREPRENEURS

A must for every entrepreneur.

Internet has drastically changed the world, especially for the new entrepreneurs. It has affected how we plan and execute our actions. Today more than half of the entrepreneurs are web entrepreneurs. If you are an entrepreneur and you are not using the internet to power your business, then you are logically far behind your abilities. The Internet is something that has equal importance in the business as it registration documents. Without it success becomes slow.

You can be a web entrepreneur or a non-web entrepreneur, but what matters is that no matter what your business is, you will find some or the other way in which internet can be used to enhance your business. Today, when the world becomes technology driven, people find themselves addicted to mobile phones and laptops. In such a scenario, reaching the world becomes much easier when you are wired to the internet.

THE WEB ENTREPRENEURS

Web Entrepreneurs are the one who creates a product or service on the internet that the world uses to solve a problem or make their task easy. Being a web entrepreneur is one the easiest one as it is the option to start a business with minimum investment and almost no paperwork hassle. Setting up an online business is so fast that skilled people get live with a business in less than 48 hours. The best part is that your age, gender, physical location or any things will not be able to prevent you from achieving your desired success. All you need is a laptop or a PC with internet connection and the skill of programming.

The most amazing thing is that web entrepreneurs are found below the age of 30. This means that the new generation is highly inspired toward entrepreneurship in the world of web. The major proportion of them is teenagers. This is the most exciting journey and these entrepreneurs are like a wizard who create something out of nothing and then within a short time the whole world starts using it as an important tool for living. These web entrepreneurs often create things that serve as the raw material for other entrepreneurs.

INTERNET FOR EXPANSION

Whatever your business is, setting up a website just adds to more value, reach and reliability. The moment we hear of a company, the first thing we do is search it on a search engine. If you find a website for it, your trust increases on it. The Internet can also be used to expand the presence of your business as you cannot have a store or office in every part of the world, but you can have an online office that can be accessed from any place on earth to view your business details and communicate with you. A website can be considered as a virtual branch office. You can also create your website in multiple languages so that where ever it is visited from, a native feeling is always delivered.

You can also create social media pages on social websites like Twitter, Facebook, Instagram, LinkedIn, etc. depending on your category and requirement. This will help you reach the right potential audience, often for free. You can take the help of video websites like YouTube and Vimeo that lets you explain and show videos of what you and your product can do. They are great ways to host high-quality videos which can be delivered at a greater speed without any cost.

INTERNET FOR MARKETING

Social media are a good tool for website, but apart from that search engines do help in marketing too. There are both free and paid options. You can optimize your page so that search engines understand what your page is about, grab the details and deliver it to the right person searching for a similar topic. This is called search engine optimization often referred to as SEO. This can be done by hiring a professional but if you can manage to do it yourself it is free. You can also write blogs and post images online that help you attract more customers.

The paid part is even much interesting. In the traditional way of advertising, what generally happens is that you pay for the advertisement and then you have no control. People may or may not see your content but the bill is fixed. On the internet, once you place an advertisement, your advertisement is shown to people, but you are charged only when someone clicks on your advertisement. This gives you full control allowing to manage your budget efficiently.

INTERNET FOR COMMUNICATION.

A phone call is good but who writes letters through post office now? We don't even wish to send a fax now. The Internet has brought in a revolution that you need to adopt. Today sending a mail takes as much time as blinking your eyes. We can send copies of documents and more. You can video conference and make discussions and demonstrations much faster. The Internet also lets you handle client sitting at the opposite side of the globe. Thus, if you are not using the internet to boost your business you will probably be far behind in your plans.

INTERNET FOR KNOWLEDGE.

If you move back to twenty years, there was no such option like a google search. Search engines existed, but they were in their early stages and making a search was not easy. In those days if you ever required to discuss a corporate plan or a legal detail, then all you had to do was to visit a Chartered Accountant or a Lawyer and then they would make you wait for long and charge you a handsome amount of fee. Moreover, it was tough for a teenager to think of a business. You had to be old enough and have a good business qualification or at least a graduate in order to survive in the world.

Things have changed a lot. All you need to do is a google search and by the time you would have reached the layer or the Accountant's firm, you already learn everything you need to know and that too for free. Your age or financial status now does not stop you from becoming the entrepreneur that you wish to become.

There are plenty of forums online that can be used to take help from the experts. The most interesting part is that you can conduct all registrations and paperwork for your business set up online that save you from the harassment. It also saves your time and money to a great extent. You can also pay bills, collect money and do a lot of things that let save time and do more of what you are great at.

* * *

BE WITH THE RIGHT PEOPLE

Your company makes the difference.

What character you develop depends on your environment. It is the people you live with who affects the kind of character you develop. Now you don't have control over whom you have grown up with, but now that you have decided to be an entrepreneur, it is your duty to change your company. Things may seem tough while making this tough call, but this is a just one among the many sacrifices that you need to make. I am not asking you to forget all your friends, but am just asking you to change your company where you spend most of your time.

To be a successful entrepreneur you need to hang around some quality people. Now what makes a person qualified has no binding rules. Yes, there are a few things that can be considered, otherwise, there is no such certificate to declare so. Here is the few check you may perform.

PEOPLE WHO MOTIVATE.

There are a few people with whom we get highly motivated while on the other hand, you start feeling upset as you spend some time with others. The people of the first type will keep telling you about how someone they know became successful and achieved their goal. They will also tell you about how you can be successful and what are the benefits of taking a risk. If you fall in trouble and then tell stories to this person, they will just tell you about how others had similar problems and how they solved it.

On the other hand, if you meet a person of the second type, then you will have lots of unsuccessful stories to hear. They instantly become your well-wisher and instantly warn you from taking any risk as they do for themselves. Still, if you are taking a risk, they keep discouraging you and by chance, if you ever get unsuccessful, they will act as if they were waiting for this moments since years, so that they can blame you, prove themselves right and tell the world.

You must try to spend time and discuss topics with people of the first type and avoid moving around with the people of the second type. Now if someone in the family or close friends circle is of the second type, then I would not ask you to forge them. That would not be logical at all, but what you can do is avoid talking business in front of them.

PEOPLE WITH EXPERIENCE

I believe that life is too short to do all the mistakes by ourselves and then gain experience from them. Now we don't have enough time to try out every possibility by ourselves nor we have enough patience for it. So it is always right to listen to ideas from and experiences from people that are not yours.

We must use our wit to do all the necessary things but to make our decision by taking into consideration, the suggestions given by others and the experiences gained by others. However, there is a point of caution. When you look at the experiences of others, then the most important thing that you must note is the reaction of people towards their failure. What made them fail and what they did after their failure and how they recovered their failure.

If you take a closer look, then you will find that people who get successful at their first attempt are not experienced enough to handle the ups and downs that come in their way, but people who had seen failures or have faced failures themselves have the courage to handle any obstacle that comes in their way.

PEOPLE WITH KNOWLEDGE

You must have noticed there where ever you go, everyone is ready to guide you with some advice of their own. Now I would not say that they are all wrong but, they are derived from their limit of knowledge. Being an entrepreneur needs the depth knowledge of your subject and thus, you must have the maximum possible knowledge. The same way, if you are taking advice from a person, make sure that the person has real knowledge and is not giving advises based on some imaginary thoughts or some fiction.

Most of the time it is seen that people with a very shallow knowledge try to impersonate as a person with deep knowledge. As a result, advice from their fanciful imagination are taken by people and people either end up doing the wrong thing or not taking the right action.

PEOPLE WHO CAN JOIN

Sooner or later as your business grows, you will need a few more helping hands to manage everything. That will be the time when you will need directors, co-founders, and employees. You can find employees based on different parameters and tests, but finding the right partners in the form of c-founders and directors is highly crucial. A right partner can double your company in a day, but a wrong partner can tear apart your company and plans. While partners support your company like you do and bring in money, resources or experience, they can also import hidden motives inside the Trojan horse. Thus, making a person your partner is not advisable unless you know them well.

So, meet with like-minded people and keep on your search for the people who can be chosen to be your partner. It may take longer, but sooner or later you will find the right person. Never make a hurry or be highly desperate and choose a wrong person.

BUSINESS ENTITIES & ASSOCIATED LAWS.

Business entities in India

Before you start your business, you must have the basic plan about who is with you, who is going to operate the business. Accordingly, you will need to form your business. There are different forms in different countries and are governed by the respective laws. However, in this section, we will deal with the different types of business entities.

You can choose to have any of them, but having a clear idea about all of them will be helpful. There may come a time, when there may be a need to migrate from one form to other. We also have a bunch of laws and bodies that govern these entities. Let's read about them one by one.

TYPES OF BUSINESS ENTITIES

The different entities are Private Ltd Company, Public Ltd Company, Unlimited Company, Sole proprietorship, Joint Hindu Family business, Partnership, Cooperatives, Limited Liability Partnership(LLP), Liaison Office, Branch Office, Project Office, Subsidiary Company.

Private Ltd Company

To form a Private Ltd company, you need to have a minimum paid up capital of Rs. 1 Lakh or such a higher amount which the government prescribes from time to time. To form such a company, you need to have a minimum of two and maximum of 50 members. These companies cannot invite the public to subscribe to its share capital and the rights of the shareholder to transfer their shares is also restricted.

Public Ltd Company

To form a Private Ltd company, you need to have a minimum paid up capital of Rs.5 Lakh or such a higher amount which the government prescribes from time to time. This company requires a minimum of seven members. There is no upper limit to the number of members who can join.

Unlimited Company
This is a form of business where the liability of all its members is unlimited. The personal assets of the members can be used to settle the debts. It can at any time re-register as a limited company under section 32 of the Companies Act.

Sole proprietorship
This is a form of business where a single person handles the entire business organization. This form of business does not form a separate business entity. The proprietor, who is the owner of the business is the sole recipient of all the all the profit and bears all the loses. There is no separate law that governs the sole proprietorship.

Partnership
The partnership is "the relation between persons who have agreed to share the profits of the business carried on by all or any one of them acting for all". It is governed by the Indian Partnership Act 1932.

Joint Hindu Family
Joint Hindu Family is a form of business organization wherein the members of the family can only own and manage the business. It is governed by Hindu Law.

One Person Company (OPC)

One Person Company which is often called an OPC is almost equivalent to a Private Limited Company with a single difference that it has only one member. This is something with some benefits of proprietorship and some power of a private limited company.

Co-Operatives

Co-operatives are a form of voluntary organization, wherein the members work together for the promotion of the interests of its members. There is no restriction to the entry or exit of any member. It is governed by Cooperative Societies Act 1912.

Limited Liability Partnership

If a company is formed under the LLP (Limited Liability Partnership) at least one member has unlimited liability while all the other members have limited liability, Limited to the extent of their contribution in the LLP. Unlike the general partnership forms, this kind of partnership does not get terminated by the death or insolvency of the limed partners. This kind of Business entity is governed by the Limited Liability Partnership Act, 2008.

Liaison Office

This is a kind of representative office which is set up to understand the business and investment environment. It is barred from taking up any commercial/industrial/trading activity and its role is limited to aggregation of information and promotion of exports/imports. It has to maintain itself out of inward remittances received from the parent company.

Branch Office

Foreign companies which are into manufacturing and trading activities abroad are permitted to set up branch offices in India for various purposes like the rendering of professional and consultancy services, export/import of goods etc. Branch offices are not permitted to carry out manufacturing activities on their own. RBI is the statutory body that grants permission to foreign companies for setting up branch offices in India.

Project Office

Foreign companies can set up temporary project offices in India for carrying out activities related to that specific project.

Subsidiary Company

In India, the sectors where 100% foreign direct investment is permitted their foreign companies can set up a wholly-owned subsidiary. The wholly-owned subsidiary can be either of the following business entities:

- Private Ltd Company
- Public Ltd Company
- Unlimited Company
- Sole Proprietorship

REGULATORY REQUIREMENTS AND STATUTORY BODIES INVOLVED IN STARTING A BUSINESS

The Companies Act 2013

The Companies act 2013 is an act of the parliament that regulates incorporation of companies, responsibilities of a company, its directors, and dissolution of the company. This act replaces the company act 1956. The companies Act 2013 introduced the One Person Company.

Ministry of Corporate Affairs

This is an Indian Government ministry that is primarily concerned with the administration of the Companies Act 2013, The companies act 1956, Limited Liability Partnership Act 2008 and other related Acts. The ministry governs the following Acts.

- The ministry administers the following acts:
- The Companies Act 2013
- The Companies Act 1956
- The Monopolies and Restrictive Trades Practices Act 1969
- The Chartered Accountant's Act 1949

- The Company Secretaries Act 1980
- Cost and Works Accountants Act 1959
- Companies Fund Act 1951
- The Indian Partnership Act 1932
- Societies Registration Act 1860
- The Companies Amendment Act 2006
- The Limited Liability Partnership Act, 2008

In August 2013, The Companies Act, 2013 was passed which replaced The Companies Act, 1956. This act was passed to regulate frauds by major corporations to avoid accounting scandals.

Ministry of Micro, Small and Medium Enterprises

Ministry of Micro, Small and Medium Enterprises is a branch of the government of India that is the apex body for formulation and administration of rules, regulating the laws relating to micro, small and medium enterprises in India.

Office of the Registrar of Companies

The responsibility of the Registrar of companies is to register companies for their state or union territories and ensure that the companies abide by the legal requirements of the Companies Act.

The Ministry of Environment and Forest

This major task of this body is to govern and ensure environmental protection, design environmental policy framework in India and undertaking conservation and survey of flora, fauna, forest, and wildlife.

The Environment Protection Act

This is an all-inclusive legislation which affirms the central government to protect the government, improve environment quality control and reduce pollution from all sources.

Reserve Bank of India(RBI)

This controls the monetary system of the country.

Security Exchange Board of India(SEBI)

This is another statutory body that controls the Indian capital market.

PROTECTING YOUR BUSINESS

Prevent your ideas from being stolen.

This may look a bit unimportant, but the fact is that this is the most important step to take. If you have a strong competitor or a betraying employee or a partner, the result of all your hard work will become equal to zero in less than a second. When you invent something, it is exactly like your child. It's your duty to protect your idea from being stolen by anyone.

When you own a property like a house, a land or a car, you register your property with some organization to keep your property protected. Those are your physical property. In the same way, your ideas, thoughts, inventions, and theories cannot be felt or held in hand, but they are still your property too. This kind of property is known as the intellectual property. Intellectual properties are easy to steal as you do not see it while being stolen and people may easily create a copy of what you make and claim themselves as the real inventor.

INTELLECTUAL PROPERTY

Intellectual property (IP)
Intellectual property refers to creations of the intellect for which a monopoly is assigned to designated owners by law.

Intellectual property rights (IPRs)
Intellectual property rights are the rights granted to the creators of IP and include trademarks, copyright, patents, industrial design rights, and in some jurisdictions trade secrets. Artistic works including music and literature, as well as discoveries, inventions, words, phrases, symbols, and designs, can all be protected as intellectual property.

Trademark
A trademark is a recognizable sign, design or expression which distinguishes products or services of a particular trader from the similar products or services of other traders. You need to submit your trademark application at the earliest to avoid any confusion and loss. Every country has its own trademark law. An international trademark law also exists. Once you file a trademark application, you may start using the TM or SM letter with your brand name or logo. This will indicate others that you have already filed an application and they should better select

some other name. The trademark process takes some time and in that meantime, you cannot go legal against anyone using your brand name, but once you receive the final confirmation and the registered trademark certificate, you may start using the alphabet R enclosed in a circle. At this time, you can file an injunction against the person using your brand name.

WHY PROTECT THE BRAND NAME AND LOGO?

It is very important, to protect your brand name and logo as that is what lets your customers identify you in the crowd. Now while you are not a big brand, or you are a well-established brand, you will always have a sword hanging near your head if your intellectual property is not trademarked.

Problems while you are not well-established.

While you are new in the business, the fear that you need to pass through is that some other rich guy may steal your idea, or use some similar idea and build a brand overnight that looks bigger than yours. In such a case, your customers will either feel that you are a sub of the other person's brand. It may also be that the other person may file a trademark application and people will start believing in them and you may soon lose your business. Now if their application is approved, you are surely in a big trouble.

The problem when you become a well-established brand.

When you get well-established and your brand becomes popular, there are multiple threats that you become prone to if your brand is not trademarked. Let me tell you about the two major problems.

People tend to imitate your business

Small brands often tend to keep their names like the big brands and sell their cheap product or service. This may bring down your customers. Not all of your customers will be smart enough to differentiate between the original and the fake source. Finally, your long-term struggle and hard work may end up getting a poor review. They may just sell what they want using your brand name in a short time span and then move away leaving a dark spot on your brand.

It may also be that your competitors may use your brand name to form a fake company, that will be used against you to bring down your good-will and productivity. Whatever be the scenario, you will be in no position to take any action if your business is not trademarked.

What if someone else copies and trademarks it?

It may also happen that someone may copy what you do and file a trademark application with the same brand name that you hold. In such a condition, you may end up paying a big amount of fine or giving up your startup for which you have given up almost everything.

HOW TO PROTECT YOUR INTELLECTUAL PROPERTY?

Apply for a Trademark

How to apply for a Trademark? This is a very simple process. You can always hire an IP Lawyer or an agent. You can also visit the nearest Intellectual property office and do it yourself if you have the basic knowledge about the trademark procedure. This is a great experience when you do it by yourself. You can simply search for the guidelines online and you will find a thousand websites that explain everything in details.

Disclose plan with limits

Here I mean to say that you may have a very big picture in your mind with lots of plans but all of them need not be disclosed to everyone. Let me divide the people around into four groups

Group 1: These will be the one who really wants your true success and you may share your concept with them but you need not disclose them in detail about how you will be executing your plan. This group will mostly consist of your parents, spouse and very close people.

Group 2: This group is your workforce that mostly consists of your employees and partners. They need to see a clear image of the vision that you hold and this would drive them to accomplish the mission. This team need not get into every detail of the task but should be very clear with the plan of action that needs to be followed.

Group 3: This is your investors who should be made aware of what you are doing and what are your future prospects but they need not know the key points that make your business successful. You need to be perfectly diplomatic, here because if you let them know too less, then they may find it insecure investing money in your business. On the other hand, if you let them know more, there are chances that your idea may get stolen. All you need to here is to act smart according to the situation.

Group 4: This is the outside world, that is full of your customers and investors, but at the same time, this world also consists of competitors and rivals. There is someone always ready to bring down your business or put you into some legal trap. To this world, you just need to show the trailer and not the movie until release.

The final conclusion that we come to is that other than you and your co-founders, there should not be anyone who should know all the parts of your business at the same time. Disclose to a person only what is relevant to their section.

THE BILLION DOLLAR IDEA

Ideas that can make you rich

I Am now going to share the last thing that is alone more important than everything else described in this book. It is about the ideas that can be put into action to make a billion-dollar, even a billion-dollar company. It is the idea that is worth everything and what makes the real difference. A right idea can change the life of may while a wrong idea can cost you your reputation, time, money, and almost everything.

So what is the billion-dollar idea?

This is a very critical question and needs to be handled properly as this is what changes the life of an Entrepreneur. So, let us not move here and there any further and simply move to the point that will take us to the idea.

The fact is that there are thousands of ideas out of which each has the potential to make at least a billion Dollar but if applied in a very right way with proper hands. Hereby proper hands I never mean experienced, or rich or artistic or anything of that short but I mean the person who has the right motivation and desire. There are a few parameters that will let you choose the right idea that would form the backbone of your company.

Firstly, identify the problem. People will not love your solution; however good it is unless they have a problem which can be solved by your solution. Now for this, what you need to do is look closely into the life of people including you and find out a problem that needs a solution. Remember, the greatest inventions have been made in this world while trying to solve own problem. If you cannot find a problem, how would you make a solution? Entrepreneurship is all about finding the best fit solution to the existing problem.

Secondly, Search for a problem in your lifestyle. If you live in a place that is a city, you should try to find the problem of people in the city and not in a remote village. Similarly, if you are an engineer and you start to find the problem of a doctor, then probably you would find some other doctor doing it better and hiring a few engineers to solve the technical part. So the idea is to stick to your native domain where you have the best capabilities to find out the problem and its solution. There must be something out in this world that you think you can do the best. If you think that there is nothing like that, then probably you have not researched enough. Every person who wishes to be an entrepreneur or have read this book up to here has at least one talent that he can do better than anyone else on the planet. Find it as that if added with an idea, will make it a billion-dollar idea.

Thirdly, start with the idea that comes to the mind. It is better to start with something than do nothing. I have seen a lot of startups who start with something, keep modifying as per the requirement and end up doing something else which is a much better option but would never have been started at the first place.

Last but not the least, start with anything that feels right. It may be decent or be complicated, but it is always worth a billion dollars if you have the passion to make it or the understanding of the knowledge. There will always be someone who will be ready to bring forward an objection or a sentence of demotivation. It is your task to avoid thinking about what they think as if you start thinking their thoughts, you are no more an entrepreneur.

Never get fooled to wait for someone to sell you or lend you a billion-dollar idea, as ideas come from scratch and any idea is worth a million dollars. It is all upon us about how far we would be able to take it. There is always a difference between looking after your own child and someone else's child. So take the very own idea that came out of your observations and has a touch of your passion and leaves no stone unturned. Mark my words, that idea would surely take you to a billion dollars or will fetch you the idea that will make you a billionaire.

CONCLUSION

This was a short journey where I have shared with you some of the important facts and some studies that can be considered while starting your own startup. I am sure that you have the fire in you to change the world with your company.

It's time to start your company no matter how. An entrepreneur never finds a road made in advance for them to proceed as entrepreneurs are the ones who invent a road. Life is tough but that should never be an excuse to stop inventing.

My final word of advice would be that never run after doing something that someone else has done and succeeded. It might fetch you a lot of money without risk but at the end of the day, you won't be inventing something. So just start inventing. You will feel awesome at the end.

Feel free to write me at talk@amitkumarjha.com

Notes

www.ingramcontent.com/pod-product-compliance
Lightning Source LLC
Chambersburg PA
CBHW031542210526
45464CB00003B/1115